S0-BUA-718

DEBT FREE

Journal

by

Daniel Meichtry

Authors Note

Like you may be, I was at a place in my life where I felt trapped by my circumstances and powerless to do anything about them. I was twenty-one years old, newly married, and my wife and I were renting a room from my parents after facing some difficulties the previous year. My wife lost her job a month after we got married; my hours were cut in half a month later; a slew of health problems arose in our family; we were living on a very limited income while trying to figure out our "adult" lives, and any chance of progress felt insurmountable under the heavy weight of our debts and expenses. And then my brother invited us over for dinner.

He and his wife had been going through the process of paying off debt with hopes of becoming "Debt Free". I'm sure I had heard of this concept before, but it didn't really hit me until that moment that it could be possible for us. After that fateful night, we were entirely committed to becoming Debt Free, and over the next 14 months my wife and I paid off all of our consumer debt. Within 6 months of becoming Debt Free, we had saved a $10,000 emergency fund, attained new jobs making almost double what we had previously made, and moved into a 2-bedroom apartment that we absolutely loved (and that didn't involve sharing a wall with my parents.)

After this focused period of being intentional with our finances, we felt like we had hit the reset button on our adult lives. Our ideology was shifting from being "victims of our current circumstances" to "choosing our own path by intentional planning and action". We felt a newfound freedom that would not only shape our financial future, but also many major life decisions.

Becoming and remaining Debt Free has been one of the most pivotal, life-changing actions I've ever taken and it has paid dividends in every corner of my family's life. After becoming Debt Free ourselves, we started to spark intrigue from friends, family members and acquaintances who had watched us along the way and wondered how we actually accomplished this feat. I have personally strategized with many of them to help them begin their own Debt Free Journey and have watched it literally transform entire family trajectories in the process!

This is where you come in. Put simply, *Debt Free Journal* was created to help you become Debt Free. Furthermore, this journal was designed to help bring clarity to where you financially stand today, help you define your debt and build an action plan to pay it off, and to create a healthy rhythm of intentionality with your personal finances to help you build a purposeful life.

Let me just say, I'm so glad you are here and genuinely believe this will be a life-changing, trajectory-altering process for you. My hope is that you look back and remember this moment as the defining point when you chose to take ownership of your personal finances, and ultimately, ownership of your life. May this be one of the last moments you feel chained by your environment and helpless to do anything about it. I hope this process gives you clarity to the reality of your circumstances and equips you to make decisions that lead you to live a more simple, purposeful and intentional life.

Here's to the journey.

Sincerely,
Daniel Meichtry

For resources to help you on your Debt Free Journey
go to www.debtfreejournal.com or email hello@debtfreejournal.com

Printed in Canada
First Printing, 2021
ISBN 978-0-9978240-3-2

CONTENTS

“If you fail to plan, you’ve planned to fail.”

BENJAMIN FRANKLIN

What will completing this journal do for me?

You will understand where you are financially, today. We will begin by discovering where you are starting from financially. For many people, this exercise will provide the clearest financial picture they have ever had in their life.

You will determine the debts you currently have, save an emergency fund and create a clear plan to become Debt Free. After understanding the debts you currently have, you will establish your emergency fund and build your debt-payoff timeline. This will create momentum as you focus your efforts toward paying off each debt, one-by-one.

You will build a new rhythm of intentionality with your finances and feel more in control of your own financial future. As you go through each week, you will pause to reflect,, acknowledge what's going well, and decide what tweaks are necessary to keep you on track. This process will help you feel more in control over your financial life on your journey to becoming Debt Free.

You can experience Debt Freedom. As you work through each week and complete the monthly reviews along the way, you will build an archive of progress along your Debt Free Journey. There will be moments to intentionally pause, assess and celebrate how far you've come on your journey; that will solidify these new habits and keep you on track to hit your goals. If you remain accountable to this journal you can experience the freedom that comes from being completely Debt Free.

YOUR WHY

According to best-selling author and professional motivator Simon Sinek, "The *why* is the purpose, cause or belief that drives every one of us." That means that behind every action you take, every habit you desire to change or goal you set out to achieve, there is a core purpose driving you. This is your *why*.

Here are some examples of others *why* statements from the #debtfreecommunity

"I never want to ask family or friends for money again. I want to be self sufficient and responsible for my own life."

"To build a better life for my children than the one that I had. I want to change my family tree."

"To never feel trapped by my circumstances."

"To stop living in fear. To never wonder how I'll buy groceries for my kids, clothe them or put a roof over their head."

The only stipulation to your *why* is that it be meaningful to YOU. It's all about what's motivating you to make this shift toward living Debt Free. On this journey you may encounter difficult stretches; you may even want to quit at times. In those moments, I would encourage you to come back to this page and remember what's driving you to get out of debt in the first place.

Why do you want to become Debt Free?

___

___

___

___

"To begin to think with purpose, is to enter the ranks of those strong ones who only recognize failure as one of the pathways to attainment."

JAMES ALLEN

Where am I today?

In order to know how to reach your destination, you first need to establish your starting point. In this section, you will gather information to establish a road map for your financial journey.

This section will potentially take the most amount of time. This could take an hour or more if starting from scratch but may take just minutes if you already have your necessary information gathered. Emerging with a clear picture of your starting point is the goal.

1. **What are my Debts?** You will lay out all of your debts and total them up to give you a clear picture of your individual debts and your debt as a whole.

2. **Do I have any Assets?** You will determine what assets you have currently and estimate their total value.

3. **What is my Net Worth?** Combining what you found in the Debt and Assets sections, you will establish what your starting Net Worth is before you embark on your Debt Free Journey.

4. **Should I have an Emergency Fund?** You will determine what size Emergency Fund is necessary and set a goal for funding it.

5. **When is my Debt Free Date?** Based on your total debt balance, how it's broken down, and the total amount you can pay toward debt each month, you will build a detailed debt-payoff timeline that will establish when to pay off each debt and when you plan to be Debt Free.

Ready?
Take a deep breath.
Let's get started.

DEBT

Debt

{det} • noun

Something that is owed or that one is bound to pay. A liability or obligation to pay something.

Tools required for this section

1. **Collect All Debts.** If you don't have all these handy, you can check debtors websites or apps, your latest statement, call your lender or use a free credit monitoring app to see your outstanding debts.

2. **Create a Budget.** It's necessary to have a monthly budget to understand your expenses and how much you can put toward debt each month. If you don't already have one made, I recommend using an app like YNAB, Every Dollar, or Mint but you can also use a written budget form if desired.

3. **A Calculator.** The one on your smartphone will do the trick. I recommend using a calculator for complete accuracy during this crucial process.

DEBT

What's the plan?

1. *List out all debts* - Include name, type, interest rate, minimum monthly required payment and the total balance. For now, you'll list these out in no particular order.

2. *Total your debts* - Sum the total balances and the minimum monthly required payment of all debts listed. The sum of your debts balances will provide your total debt balance or your Debt Free number. The sum of your minimum monthly payments will show how much money you are already paying toward debt each month.

3. *Determine how much extra you can put toward debt each month* - You now know how much you are required to pay, but now you need to determine how much extra is left in your monthly budget to put towards paying your debt off as quickly as possible. This extra amount will be the main accelerator to becoming Debt Free as quickly as possible.

DEBT

Date / /

List Your Debts

This includes, but is not limited to credit cards, vehicles, personal loans, school loans, medical bills, back taxes or any other form of money you owe to an institution or individual.

Name	Type	Int %	Min	Balance

DEBT

Name	Type	Int %	Min	Balance

Debt Totals

Total Monthly Minimum

Extra Monthly Toward Debt

Total Monthly Debt Payment

Total Debt Balance

ASSETS

Assets

{as-sets} • *noun*

Owned items of value including cash, investments, vehicles and property.

Tools required for this section

1. **Collect Current Asset Values.** Depending on the asset, you should be able to get this from bank or investment apps/websites, statements or online estimators (for assets such as vehicles or properties).

2. **A Calculator.** For accuracy, use a simple calculator, such as the one on your smartphone, to complete this section.

What's the plan?

1. ***List out all your assets*** - List each asset's name and its current estimated value. Once all assets are collected, total their estimated value. This is essential for completing the Net Worth section just ahead.

ASSETS

Date / /

Assets List

This includes, but is not limited to: cash, stocks, retirement accounts, vehicles, property and other items of considerable value.

	Name	Est. Value
1.		
2.		
3.		
4.		
5.		
6.		
7.		
8.		
9.		
10.		
11.		
12.		
13.		
14.		

Total Assets Value

____

NET WORTH

Net Worth

{net-wurth} • *noun*

The total assets minus total debts of an individual.

Tools required for this section

1. **Total Debts & Asset Values.** Take these from the Debt and Assets sections you just completed.

2. **A Calculator.** For accuracy, use a simple calculator, such as the one on your smartphone, to complete this section.

What's the plan?

1. *Net Worth Calculation* - Now that you have the total value of your assets and your total debt balance collected, simply subtract your total debt balance from your total assets value to determine your Net Worth. This will be one of the most important numbers to track progress throughout your Debt Free Journey.

**At this point, it's normal for this number to be negative. It might be a bit scary, but watching your Net Worth hit $0 and then grow is part of the joy of this journey. Just be patient.*

NET WORTH

Date / /

EXAMPLE NET WORTH

Subtract

Total Debt Balance

$100,00

From

Total Assets Value

$50,00

To Find Your

Net Worth

– $50,00

Subtract

Total Debt Balance

From

Total Assets Value

To Find Your

Net Worth

EMERGENCY FUND

Emergency Fund

{ə'mərjənsē fənd} • *noun*

A predetermined sum of money set aside for unexpected expenses and hardships.

Have you ever been caught off guard financially? Maybe your car breaks down. You break a bone and have to miss work for a time. You lose your job without notice. Your dishwasher leaks and floods your kitchen. Listen up, if there is one thing I can guarantee you, it's that you will not perfectly predict every expense that comes your way. Expenses will come up that you didn't plan for. The way you handle these situations can look drastically different depending on how prepared you are. If you're living paycheck to paycheck, lacking a monthly budget and depending on your credit card to bail you out, these surprises will be stressful and set you back dramatically. But what if you had a buffer?

Having an Emergency Fund is kind of like wearing a seatbelt. You don't put your seatbelt on when you need it, you put it on before you even start driving your car. The same should be true when preparing for an emergency. You won't be prepared for an emergency if you wait until it strikes to save for it, you need to have a plan in advance. That's why it's best to start your Emergency Fund before you begin your Debt Free Journey.

Emergencies don't have to cripple you or derail your Debt Free Journey, but in order to deal with them you do need to be prepared. This is where an Emergency Fund comes in. Your Emergency Fund is your buffer during your Debt Free Journey. According to a 2019 GOBankingRates survey, almost 70% of Americans have less than $1,000 in savings and an astonishing

EMERGENCY FUND

45% have nothing saved. One of the biggest obstacles to becoming Debt Free is creating new debt because you are caught unprepared for an unexpected emergency.

Before you start paying off debts, you should establish a modest Emergency Fund. This does not need to be a huge amount to start, but enough to cover you in a bind. For most, this will be somewhere between $1,000 and $10,000 dollars. If you have 3 kids and live in Manhattan, your circumstance will necessitate a larger Emergency Fund than if you're single and living in Louisville. As a rule of thumb, we recommend at least one month of fixed expenses (housing, utilities, insurance, food, etc.) to start out and up to three months while you are working to become Debt Free. Using your budget, you should quickly be able to determine your fixed living costs each month and multiply it by the number of months you deem necessary for your Emergency Fund.

It's important the amount of this Emergency Fund isn't so large that it is unattainable and keeps you from getting started on paying off debts, but isn't so small that it doesn't actually protect you from slipping back into debt if a minor emergency strikes. You can always adjust this amount along your journey as necessary. For now, determine what amount is right for you and save this up as quickly as possible to provide a firm foundation to start your Debt Free Journey.

Emergency Fund

Emergency Fund Amount ______________________

Fund by Date ______________________

TIMELINE

Timeline

{'tīm - 'līn} • *noun*

The schedule in which you plan to pay off each of your debts and become Debt Free.

Tools required for this section

1. **Debt Totals.** These totals will come from the previous *Debt* section and are necessary to complete your debt payoff timeline.

2. **Debt Timeline Calculator.** For ease of use and accuracy while establishing your timeline, we suggest using a free online tool to help with this important part of the process. Check out some of our favorite debt payoff timeline calculators at www.debtfreejournal.com

TIMELINE

What's the plan?

1. ***Use an online debt timeline tool*** *- Using the information from the previous section, determine the total amount you can pay toward debt each month, the order that you will attack each debt and how quickly you can become Debt Free.*

2. ***Determine your debt payoff order*** - The most prominent methodologies are the Debt Snowball or Debt Avalanche (both explained below.) You may have a specific reason to pay your debts off in another order and that's okay. Choose what you think is best for your situation, but remember to focus on one debt at a time as you pay them off.

3. ***Your Debt Free Date*** - This is a hugely defining moment! You now have a strategy to payoff your debts and your Debt Free Date. Getting to this point is already a big milestone. You are almost ready to start attacking your debts.

Debt Snowball

Pay off debts one at a time, from smallest total amount to largest total amount. This method focuses primarily on momentum as you will get quick wins as you pay off each debt. This is our preferred approach.

Debt Avalanche

Pay off debts one at a time, from highest interest to lowest interest. This method focuses on trying to save you the most amount of interest, but for many this is a more difficult approach.

TIMELINE

Date / /

Debt Payoff Order

Using the Debt Snowball, Avalanche, or your own method, list your debts in the order you intend to pay them off and include the desired payoff date and current balance of each debt. Don't worry, this plan may change over time. If there is a major change in your projected timeline, you can always come back to this page and recalculate your timeline.

	Name	Payoff Date	Current Balance
1.			
2.			
3.			
4.			
5.			
6.			
7.			
8.			
9.			
10.			
11.			
12.			
13.			
14.			
15.			

TIMELINE

	Name	Payoff Date	Current Balance
16.			
17.			
18.			
19.			
20.			
21.			
22.			
23.			
24.			
25.			
26.			
27.			
28.			

Debt Free Timeline

Current Debt Balance

____

Debt Free Date

____

Weekly Journal

Introduction

Each week, you will check in to answer a few questions, assess how your week went, refocus on your current debt payoff goal and build a plan for the following week. This weekly journal will help build a rhythm of accountability to your budget and toward systematically reaching each debt payoff. It will also instill the discipline necessary to help you reach your goal of becoming Debt Free.

1. **Weekly Questions.** Each week, there are four questions designed to keep your budget on track, celebrate wins and acknowledge missteps, determine if any habits are causing an issue, and pause to consider any upcoming financial decisions you need to make.

2. **Weekly Journal.** This will serve as a marker for the week you just finished and a launching pad for the week ahead. As you assess the previous week, you will state one thing you are grateful for and rate the week. Then you'll look at the week ahead and list any upcoming financial tasks you might need to complete.

3. **Primary Debt Payoff.** Focus is key as you pay each debt off, one-by-one. Keep your eye on the prize by stating the primary debt you are currently paying off. Once one debt is paid off, you will move onto attacking the next debt on your timeline.

"Motivation is what gets you started. Habit is what keeps you going."

JIM ROHN

WEEKLY
Journal

1 / 1 / 21

1. Did I have any financial wins this week?
   - Under budget for groceries.
   - Sold some extra clothes on Poshmark.
   - Paid $100 extra toward my car loan.
   - Picked up an extra shift and made $150.

2. Did I have any financial fails this week?
   - Went to an impromptu Happy Hour and spent $30 that wasn't budgeted.
   - Bought some running shoes that cost more than what I had planned.

3. Do I need to adjust my budget or habits this week?
   - Update budget for extra income and added expenses.
   - No buying unplanned items.
   - Say no to outings that aren't budgeted or I can't afford.

4. Do I have any big financial decisions to consider this week?
   - Determine if I can afford friends weekend cabin trip in March and let them know.
   - Need to officially call and close recently paid off credit card.

WEEKLY

Journal

This week, I'm grateful for...

Supportive friends and family

Rate This Week

1 2 3 4 5 6 (7) 8 9 10

Why did you give that rating?

Made some extra income but need to be better about saying "no".

Action Items

Are there any bills, debt payments, or other financial tasks I need to tackle this week?

- [x] Cancel my streaming subscription
- [ ] Email car insurance about checking for better rates
- [ ] Call and close paid off credit card
- [ ] Make extra $150 payment on car loan
- [ ]

Primary Debt Payoff

Name: 2015 Toyota Corolla

Balance: $3,500 Payoff Date: April 2021

WEEKLY
Journal

/ /

1. Did I have any financial wins this week?

2. Did I have any financial fails this week?

3. Do I need to adjust my budget or habits this week?

4. Do I have any big financial decisions to consider this week?

WEEKLY
Journal

This week, I'm grateful for...

____

Rate This Week

1 2 3 4 5 6 7 8 9 10

Why did you give that rating?

____

____

Action Items

Are there any bills, debt payments, or other financial tasks I need to tackle this week?

- ○ ________________________________
- ○ ________________________________
- ○ ________________________________
- ○ ________________________________
- ○ ________________________________

Primary Debt Payoff

Name: ________________________________

Balance: ________________ Payoff Date: ________________

WEEKLY
Journal

/ /

1. Did I have any financial wins this week?

2. Did I have any financial fails this week?

3. Do I need to adjust my budget or habits this week?

4. Do I have any big financial decisions to consider this week?

WEEKLY
Journal

This week, I'm grateful for...

___

Rate This Week

1 2 3 4 5 6 7 8 9 10

Why did you give that rating?

___

___

Action Items

Are there any bills, debt payments, or other financial tasks I need to tackle this week?

- ○ ___
- ○ ___
- ○ ___
- ○ ___
- ○ ___

Primary Debt Payoff

Name: ___

Balance: ___ Payoff Date: ___

WEEKLY
Journal

/ /

1. Did I have any financial wins this week?

2. Did I have any financial fails this week?

3. Do I need to adjust my budget or habits this week?

4. Do I have any big financial decisions to consider this week?

WEEKLY
Journal

This week, I'm grateful for...

____

Rate This Week

1 2 3 4 5 6 7 8 9 10

Why did you give that rating?

____

____

Action Items

Are there any bills, debt payments, or other financial tasks I need to tackle this week?

- ○ ______________________________
- ○ ______________________________
- ○ ______________________________
- ○ ______________________________
- ○ ______________________________

Primary Debt Payoff

Name: ______________________________

Balance: ______________ Payoff Date: ______________

WEEKLY
Journal

/ /

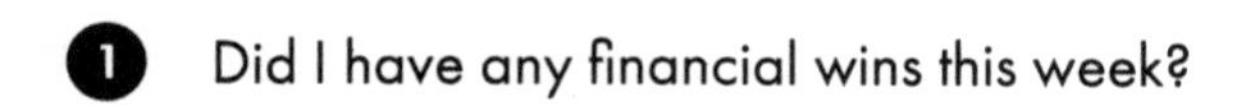

1. Did I have any financial wins this week?

2. Did I have any financial fails this week?

3. Do I need to adjust my budget or habits this week?

4. Do I have any big financial decisions to consider this week?

WEEKLY
Journal

This week, I'm grateful for...

____

Rate This Week

1 2 3 4 5 6 7 8 9 10

Why did you give that rating?

____

____

Action Items

Are there any bills, debt payments, or other financial tasks I need to tackle this week?

- ○ ____
- ○ ____
- ○ ____
- ○ ____
- ○ ____

Primary Debt Payoff

Name: ____

Balance: ____________________ Payoff Date: ____________________

Monthly Review

Introduction

At the end of each month you will take a moment to pause and reflect on your progress. Start by reading a principle that will help guide you on your Debt Free Journey, then assess and reset your budget, and finish by reviewing your progress for the month.

1. **Financial Principles.** At the end of each month, you will dive into a single financial principle. These will become the pillars of your financial vocabulary and help you to build a well rounded understanding of how-to manage your personal finances well.

2. **Monthly Questions.** Each month, there will be two additional questions centered around your budget. This is the perfect time to assess how the previous month went, determine what needs to change to be successful in the coming month and to set up next month's budget.

3. **Progress Review.** Tracking progress and acknowledging movement each month is paramount in building momentum as you move closer to your goal of becoming Debt Free. You will end your review by calculating your debt totals, allowing you to see your progress from month to month.

"Follow effective action with quiet reflection. From the quiet reflection will come even more effective action."

PETER DRUCKER

STEWARDSHIP

The careful and responsible management of something entrusted to one's care.

One month down. Well done! By this point, you will have established where you stand financially, you have a debt-payoff timeline and Debt Free Date, and you have started the weekly rhythm of journaling. Heck, you might have even paid off a debt!

Now you may be thinking, "Why would this be the opportune time to talk about this thing called stewardship?" From my experience, the sooner you begin to see your finances as something to steward, the faster you will transition your mindset from being a victim of your circumstances to taking ownership of your financial decisions. This is an essential transition to make as you build the foundation of your financial future.

When you start to see your finances through the lens of stewardship, it gives you permission to make the right decisions at the right time. After all, if your income, debt, circumstances, choices, and actions are all entrusted to you for careful and responsible management then it becomes your duty to make the most of your personal finances. That means when your friends invite you to happy hour for the second time this week, or to take that unplanned trip to the "insert instagrammable, tropical destination" with zero notice, or when that item you didn't need goes on sale, you have permission to say NO because it's not in line with the plan you've committed to.

If you haven't found out by now, this will be a huge part of your success or stagnation in this process. On your Debt Free Journey you will feel like you're saying "no" a lot, but you have to remember what you are saying "yes" to - your *why*. Your *why* from the beginning of this journal will empower you to steward your finances with greater intention while you make the inevitable tough decisions ahead.

You will have weeks when you don't feel like picking up this journal, when you want to skip entering that expense into the budget for $26.32 to Taco Bell, or when you are tempted to buy an eleventh pair of shoes instead of making a $200 payment toward your student loans. I get it, I've been there too. You may have moments where shame and guilt attempt to steal your integrity, but in order for this journal - and your journey - to be effective, you have to be honest. When you are honest about your shortcomings, they become opportunities for progress. Good stewardship requires honesty, integrity, responsibility, and commitment. If this concept is newer for you and you don't have it down just yet, that's okay! What matters is forward progress and momentum. One foot in front of the other. You got this.

MONTHLY

Review

1 / 29 / 21

1. Review last month's budget. Did anything catch me off guard or not go as planned last month?

- Budget more for groceries.
- Less eating out.
- No new clothes this month.

2. Layout next month's budget. Do any categories need to change or are there any special considerations (birthdays, trips, events, expenses) this coming month?

- Nieces Birthday is on the 15th. Budget $20 for gift.
- Save $150 toward friends cabin trip in March.
- Add water utility bill for $100 (every other month).

Progress Review

How much did I pay toward debt this month?

$1,200

What's the total amount I've paid toward debt?

$7,400

How much debt do I have left until I'm Debt Free?

$19,800

When is my Debt Free Date?

April 2022

STEWARDSHIP

The careful and responsible management of something entrusted to one's care.

One month down. Well done! By this point, you will have established where you stand financially, you have a debt-payoff timeline and Debt Free Date, and you have started the weekly rhythm of journaling. Heck, you might have even paid off a debt!

Now you may be thinking, "Why would this be the opportune time to talk about this thing called stewardship?" From my experience, the sooner you begin to see your finances as something to steward, the faster you will transition your mindset from being a victim of your circumstances to taking ownership of your financial decisions. This is an essential transition to make as you build the foundation of your financial future.

When you start to see your finances through the lens of stewardship, it gives you permission to make the right decisions at the right time. After all, if your income, debt, circumstances, choices, and actions are all entrusted to you for careful and responsible management then it becomes your duty to make the most of your personal finances. That means when your friends invite you to happy hour for the second time this week, or to take that unplanned trip to the "insert instagrammable, tropical destination" with zero notice, or when that item you didn't need goes on sale, you have permission to say NO because it's not in line with the plan you've committed to.

If you haven't found out by now, this will be a huge part of your success or stagnation in this process. On your Debt Free Journey you will feel like you're saying "no" a lot, but you have to remember what you are saying "yes" to - your *why*. Your *why* from the beginning of this journal will empower you to steward your finances with greater intention while you make the inevitable tough decisions ahead.

You will have weeks when you don't feel like picking up this journal, when you want to skip entering that expense into the budget for $26.32 to Taco Bell, or when you are tempted to buy an eleventh pair of shoes instead of making a $200 payment toward your student loans. I get it, I've been there too. You may have moments where shame and guilt attempt to steal your integrity, but in order for this journal - and your journey - to be effective, you have to be honest. When you are honest about your shortcomings, they become opportunities for progress. Good stewardship requires honesty, integrity, responsibility, and commitment. If this concept is newer for you and you don't have it down just yet, that's okay! What matters is forward progress and momentum. One foot in front of the other. You got this.

MONTHLY

Review

/ /

1. Review last month's budget. Did anything catch me off guard or not go as planned last month?

2. Layout next month's budget. Do any categories need to change or are there any special considerations (birthdays, trips, events, expenses) this coming month?

Progress Review

How much did I pay toward debt this month?

____

What's the total amount I've paid toward debt?

____

How much debt do I have left until I'm Debt Free?

____

When is my Debt Free Date?

____

WEEKLY
Journal

/ /

1. Did I have any financial wins this week?

2. Did I have any financial fails this week?

3. Do I need to adjust my budget or habits this week?

4. Do I have any big financial decisions to consider this week?

WEEKLY

Journal

This week, I'm grateful for...

____

Rate This Week

1 2 3 4 5 6 7 8 9 10

Why did you give that rating?

____

____

Action Items

Are there any bills, debt payments, or other financial tasks I need to tackle this week?

- ○ ______________________________
- ○ ______________________________
- ○ ______________________________
- ○ ______________________________
- ○ ______________________________

Primary Debt Payoff

Name: ______________________________

Balance: ______________ Payoff Date: ______________

WEEKLY
Journal

/ /

1. Did I have any financial wins this week?

2. Did I have any financial fails this week?

3. Do I need to adjust my budget or habits this week?

4. Do I have any big financial decisions to consider this week?

WEEKLY
Journal

This week, I'm grateful for...

____

Rate This Week

1 2 3 4 5 6 7 8 9 10

Why did you give that rating?

____

____

Action Items

Are there any bills, debt payments, or other financial tasks I need to tackle this week?

- ○ ____
- ○ ____
- ○ ____
- ○ ____
- ○ ____

Primary Debt Payoff

Name: ____

Balance: ____________________ Payoff Date: ____________________

WEEKLY

Journal

/ /

1. Did I have any financial wins this week?

2. Did I have any financial fails this week?

3. Do I need to adjust my budget or habits this week?

4. Do I have any big financial decisions to consider this week?

WEEKLY
Journal

This week, I'm grateful for...

____

Rate This Week

1 2 3 4 5 6 7 8 9 10

Why did you give that rating?

____

____

Action Items

Are there any bills, debt payments, or other financial tasks I need to tackle this week?

- ○ ____
- ○ ____
- ○ ____
- ○ ____
- ○ ____

Primary Debt Payoff

Name: ____

Balance: ____________________ Payoff Date: ____________________

WEEKLY
Journal

/ /

1. Did I have any financial wins this week?

2. Did I have any financial fails this week?

3. Do I need to adjust my budget or habits this week?

4. Do I have any big financial decisions to consider this week?

WEEKLY
Journal

This week, I'm grateful for...

____

Rate This Week

1 2 3 4 5 6 7 8 9 10

Why did you give that rating?

____

____

Action Items

Are there any bills, debt payments, or other financial tasks I need to tackle this week?

- ○ ____
- ○ ____
- ○ ____
- ○ ____
- ○ ____

Primary Debt Payoff

Name: ____

Balance: ____________________ Payoff Date: ____________________

BUDGETING

The process of planning estimated income and expenses for a set period of time.

Here we are. The dreaded "B" word. The big, bad, hairy, ugly, I-don't-wanna-do-it, maybe it's just not for me - budget.

I'll be honest. Budgeting is probably the most avoided part of stewarding your personal finances. When friends ask me to share our story of how we became debt free, I start to completely lose them when I begin talking about the importance of sticking to a monthly budget. I get it. The discipline of building a budget, tracking all of your expenses, reconciling your missteps, and repeating this month after month does not sound very exhilarating. However, a written, monthly budget is the single most important tool to stewarding your finances well and specifically, to helping you become Debt Free. Let me explain...

Your budget is your "source of truth" document made each month that lists the expenses you have planned (things like rent, transportation, food, clothing, entertainment, insurance, debt, planned savings, giving, investing etc.) and your expected income. The framework for your budget can be as general or specific as is effective for you, as long as it accurately reflects your income and expenses at the end of the month. When you create your first budget, you might even find that your expenses outweigh your income. Ouch. If this catches you by surprise, there's a good chance you've been living outside of your means or that your income is not sufficient to maintain it. That may be why your budget is flipped on its head.

Your budget is the accountability tool that will keep you honest throughout your Debt Free Journey and beyond. It provides an objective, third party ledger to say, "Bud, the way you feel about your money and the reality of it just aren't adding up. We have some things to fix here." This is why it's so powerful! It's not because it's complicated or daunting in nature, it's that it actually forces you to deal with your lifestyle and spending habits, and this can be an uncomfortable process at first. Probably because it reveals a lot more about your life than just your monthly expenses.

All that to say, it does get easier. My wife and I have stuck to a written budget for over seven years. While it's not always easy, it is much easier than when we first started. We still have missteps and adjustments, and we are far from perfect, but we are committed to our monthly budget because it works. Your budget will likely prove to be your most vital tool on your Debt Free Journey. So if you've been struggling with finding your groove with your budget, do not give up. Adjust, adapt, and keep getting after it until your budget becomes a steady practice that consistently serves your goal of becoming Debt Free.

MONTHLY

Review

/ /

1. Review last month's budget. Did anything catch me off guard or not go as planned last month?

2. Layout next month's budget. Do any categories need to change or are there any special considerations (birthdays, trips, events, expenses) this coming month?

Progress Review

How much did I pay toward debt this month?

____

What's the total amount I've paid toward debt?

____

How much debt do I have left until I'm Debt Free?

____

When is my Debt Free Date?

____

WEEKLY
Journal

/ /

1. Did I have any financial wins this week?

2. Did I have any financial fails this week?

3. Do I need to adjust my budget or habits this week?

4. Do I have any big financial decisions to consider this week?

WEEKLY
Journal

This week, I'm grateful for...

____

Rate This Week

1 2 3 4 5 6 7 8 9 10

Why did you give that rating?

____

____

Action Items

Are there any bills, debt payments, or other financial tasks I need to tackle this week?

○ ____

○ ____

○ ____

○ ____

○ ____

Primary Debt Payoff

Name: ____

Balance: ____________________ Payoff Date: ____________________

WEEKLY
Journal

/ /

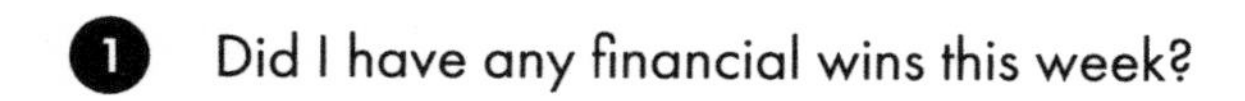

1. Did I have any financial wins this week?

2. Did I have any financial fails this week?

3. Do I need to adjust my budget or habits this week?

4. Do I have any big financial decisions to consider this week?

WEEKLY
Journal

This week, I'm grateful for...

____

Rate This Week

1 2 3 4 5 6 7 8 9 10

Why did you give that rating?

____

____

Action Items

Are there any bills, debt payments, or other financial tasks I need to tackle this week?

○ ____

○ ____

○ ____

○ ____

○ ____

Primary Debt Payoff

Name: ____

Balance: ____________________ Payoff Date: ____________________

WEEKLY
Journal

/ /

1. Did I have any financial wins this week?

2. Did I have any financial fails this week?

3. Do I need to adjust my budget or habits this week?

4. Do I have any big financial decisions to consider this week?

WEEKLY

Journal

This week, I'm grateful for...

____

Rate This Week

1 2 3 4 5 6 7 8 9 10

Why did you give that rating?

____

____

Action Items

Are there any bills, debt payments, or other financial tasks I need to tackle this week?

- ○ ____
- ○ ____
- ○ ____
- ○ ____
- ○ ____

Primary Debt Payoff

Name: ______________________________________

Balance: ________________ Payoff Date: ________________

WEEKLY
Journal

/ /

1. Did I have any financial wins this week?

2. Did I have any financial fails this week?

3. Do I need to adjust my budget or habits this week?

4. Do I have any big financial decisions to consider this week?

WEEKLY
Journal

This week, I'm grateful for...

Rate This Week

1 2 3 4 5 6 7 8 9 10

Why did you give that rating?

Action Items

Are there any bills, debt payments, or other financial tasks I need to tackle this week?

Primary Debt Payoff

Name:

Balance: Payoff Date:

RESILIENCE

The capacity to recover quickly from difficulties; toughness, grit.

I wrote this book in the year 2020. Yep. That 2020. Ya know, the one where the world flipped on its head from a global pandemic? The one where seemingly overnight businesses closed, everyone wore masks, and people were afraid to leave the house or see their friends and family. The year that millions of people lost their jobs without notice. The year where many, including myself, watched their retirement accounts and other investments in the stock market plummet 40% in a matter of weeks with fears it might not rebound. Even as I write this, we are still in the throws of this pandemic and not quite back to the "normal" we've always known.

Pretty grim stuff, huh? The reason I seek to vividly capture this moment is because it is just that, a moment. A season perhaps, but not the entirety of our lives. It would be easy to sit in this moment and think, "Everything I've worked toward for years has been a total waste. There's no coming back from this. I might as well just throw in the towel." And while I know it can be tempting to quit when you're down, I want to encourage you with these powerful words from Mary Pickford, "You may have a fresh start any moment you choose, for this thing that we call 'failure' is not the falling down, but the staying down." When you fall down or fall behind, but still choose to get back up and keep pressing on - that is resilience.

Now I'm aware that many people reading this took some devastating blows in 2020 and if that's you, I'm truly sorry that you had to face such a difficult season. And while a year like that may be unprecedented in its own way, seasons of hardship are not new and this will not be the last difficult season that you face in life. As painful as these moments can be while you're enduring them, these are often the moments that define us. The moments that produce toughness and grit. Such defining moments remind us that we can be resurrected from rock bottom to reach new heights.

All this to say, you will likely experience some falling down on your journey. I intentionally use the word "journey" often because as you know, this pursuit of becoming Debt Free is not a sprint, it's a marathon. You will grow weary, and the aches and pains from running long slow miles will intensify. Sometimes your falling down might be a result of your own choices, but other times it might be caused by external factors that are out of your control. And your journey is not only about the finish line, it's about the hard lessons you learn along the way that will end up shaping your vision and response to future obstacles.

Resilience invites you to get back up and keep running the race; don't let your falling down or slowing down become your final chapter. In the words of Bruce Lee, "Fall down nine times get up ten."

MONTHLY

Review

/ /

1. Review last month's budget. Did anything catch me off guard or not go as planned last month?

2. Layout next month's budget. Do any categories need to change or are there any special considerations (birthdays, trips, events, expenses) this coming month?

Progress Review

How much did I pay toward debt this month?

What's the total amount I've paid toward debt?

How much debt do I have left until I'm Debt Free?

When is my Debt Free Date?

THREE MONTHS DOWN!

Way to go! On this next page you are going to create a visual of your progress. As you flip through your journal, this will continue to remind you of the progress you've made and how much closer you are to becoming Debt Free!

Idea: *Set $50 aside this month to treat yourself. Take a moment to enjoy the fruits of your labor by doing something you normally wouldn't splurge on as you pay off debt. Let it be a reminder of your hard work and a symbol of the things you can regularly enjoy once you're Debt Free.*

QUARTERLY
Check-in

/ /

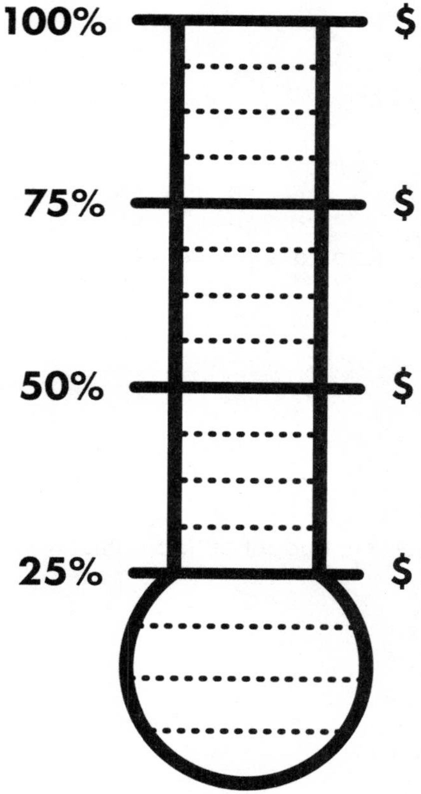

100% $

75% $

50% $

25% $

Debt Free Date

WEEKLY
Journal

/ /

1. Did I have any financial wins this week?

2. Did I have any financial fails this week?

3. Do I need to adjust my budget or habits this week?

4. Do I have any big financial decisions to consider this week?

WEEKLY
Journal

This week, I'm grateful for...

____

Rate This Week

1 2 3 4 5 6 7 8 9 10

Why did you give that rating?

____

____

Action Items

Are there any bills, debt payments, or other financial tasks I need to tackle this week?

- ○ ____
- ○ ____
- ○ ____
- ○ ____
- ○ ____

Primary Debt Payoff

Name: ____

Balance: ____________________ Payoff Date: ____________________

WEEKLY
Journal

/ /

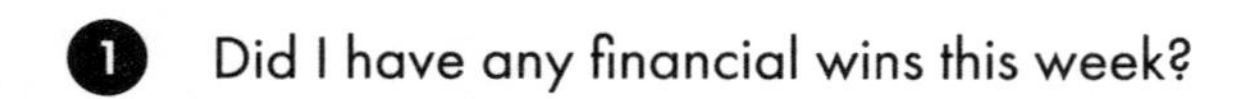

1. Did I have any financial wins this week?

2. Did I have any financial fails this week?

3. Do I need to adjust my budget or habits this week?

4. Do I have any big financial decisions to consider this week?

WEEKLY
Journal

This week, I'm grateful for...

____

Rate This Week

1 2 3 4 5 6 7 8 9 10

Why did you give that rating?

____

____

Action Items

Are there any bills, debt payments, or other financial tasks I need to tackle this week?

- ○ ______________________________
- ○ ______________________________
- ○ ______________________________
- ○ ______________________________
- ○ ______________________________

Primary Debt Payoff

Name: ______________________________

Balance: ______________ Payoff Date: ______________

WEEKLY
Journal

/ /

1. Did I have any financial wins this week?

2. Did I have any financial fails this week?

3. Do I need to adjust my budget or habits this week?

4. Do I have any big financial decisions to consider this week?

WEEKLY
Journal

This week, I'm grateful for...

____

Rate This Week

1 2 3 4 5 6 7 8 9 10

Why did you give that rating?

____

____

Action Items

Are there any bills, debt payments, or other financial tasks I need to tackle this week?

- ○ ______________________________
- ○ ______________________________
- ○ ______________________________
- ○ ______________________________
- ○ ______________________________

Primary Debt Payoff

Name: ______________________________

Balance: ______________ Payoff Date: ______________

WEEKLY
Journal

/ /

1. Did I have any financial wins this week?

2. Did I have any financial fails this week?

3. Do I need to adjust my budget or habits this week?

4. Do I have any big financial decisions to consider this week?

WEEKLY
Journal

This week, I'm grateful for...

____

Rate This Week

1 2 3 4 5 6 7 8 9 10

Why did you give that rating?

____

____

Action Items

Are there any bills, debt payments, or other financial tasks I need to tackle this week?

- ○ ______________________________
- ○ ______________________________
- ○ ______________________________
- ○ ______________________________
- ○ ______________________________

Primary Debt Payoff

Name: ______________________________

Balance: ______________ Payoff Date: ______________

DISCIPLINE

The ability to carefully control the way that you work, live, or behave, especially to achieve a goal.

At the age of 27, I weighed 300 pounds. I had high blood pressure and my doctor told me I was at risk for a major heart event in my early forties. I was pretty terrified. Throughout my life I have always had a complicated relationship with food, and my weight and overall health has been all over the map. But this news hit differently. I was a new dad now, so my health wasn't just about me. I wanted to live to walk my daughter down the aisle, have grandkids, and enjoy a healthy life in the process. I was confronted with the thought that my bad health choices might hold me back from some of life's greatest joys.

My doctor suggested that I start taking blood pressure medication and try to lose some weight. In my reluctance to take medication the rest of my life, I asked if I could fix the actual issue through healthier lifestyle choices. He smirked and said, "Sure. That would be the best way to do it. The problem is, most patients would never make the changes needed to actually fix the problem." I told him that I wasn't "most patients." I was determined to discipline my actions to a healthier lifestyle instead of masking the symptoms of my actual problem. My prescription was essentially this, eat lots of plants and don't eat meat or dairy. Basically, the opposite of my diet at the time. He closed with suggesting reading a book called 'How Not to Die,'' which convinced me to fully commit to a whole food, plant-based diet.

There is a Bible verse in the book of Hebrews that says, "discipline isn't pleasant while you're in it, but actually painful" (Hebrews 12:11). My new disciplined diet was unpleasant and painful. For the first few weeks my body had to adjust to eating food that I thought tasted horrible. But over time, it got easier. My taste buds adapted and I actually began to enjoy fruits and vegetables instead of craving a juicy burger. In one month, I lost 20lbs! That progress motivated me to keep going, and after eight months I had lost 80lbs and was healthier than I had ever been in my life. I felt like a new person. To this day, I still eat a mostly plant-based diet and have maintained my weight loss.

I'm not telling you that you need to become a vegan - I'm pretty sure most of you would close this journal immediately if I did. I am telling you that discipline can be like a superpower hidden in plain sight, disguised as boring and repetitive hard work. The discipline I was able to depend on in my weight loss journey was first learned on my journey to becoming Debt Free: keeping a budget, learning to say no, changing my bad habits and stewarding my money well each day.

The more you become disciplined with your finances, the more you will become disciplined, diligent, and discerning in other areas of your life. I consider discipline to be the single greatest mechanism for achieving my own goals. Perhaps your Debt Free Journey will also be a catalyst for monumental changes in other areas of your life. One thing is for certain, when you practice the principle of discipline, you will continually bear its fruits for the rest of your life.

MONTHLY

Review

/ /

1. Review last month's budget. Did anything catch me off guard or not go as planned last month?

2. Layout next month's budget. Do any categories need to change or are there any special considerations (birthdays, trips, events, expenses) this coming month?

Progress Review

How much did I pay toward debt this month?

____

What's the total amount I've paid toward debt?

____

How much debt do I have left until I'm Debt Free?

____

When is my Debt Free Date?

____

WEEKLY
Journal

/ /

1. Did I have any financial wins this week?

2. Did I have any financial fails this week?

3. Do I need to adjust my budget or habits this week?

4. Do I have any big financial decisions to consider this week?

WEEKLY
Journal

This week, I'm grateful for...

____

Rate This Week

1 2 3 4 5 6 7 8 9 10

Why did you give that rating?

____

____

Action Items

Are there any bills, debt payments, or other financial tasks I need to tackle this week?

- ○ ______________________________
- ○ ______________________________
- ○ ______________________________
- ○ ______________________________
- ○ ______________________________

Primary Debt Payoff

Name: ______________________________

Balance: ______________ Payoff Date: ______________

WEEKLY
Journal

/ /

1. Did I have any financial wins this week?

2. Did I have any financial fails this week?

3. Do I need to adjust my budget or habits this week?

4. Do I have any big financial decisions to consider this week?

WEEKLY
Journal

This week, I'm grateful for...

____

Rate This Week

1 2 3 4 5 6 7 8 9 10

Why did you give that rating?

____

____

Action Items

Are there any bills, debt payments, or other financial tasks I need to tackle this week?

- ○ ____
- ○ ____
- ○ ____
- ○ ____
- ○ ____

Primary Debt Payoff

Name: ____

Balance: ____________________ **Payoff Date:** ____________________

WEEKLY
Journal

/ /

1. Did I have any financial wins this week?

2. Did I have any financial fails this week?

3. Do I need to adjust my budget or habits this week?

4. Do I have any big financial decisions to consider this week?

WEEKLY
Journal

This week, I'm grateful for...

___

Rate This Week

1 2 3 4 5 6 7 8 9 10

Why did you give that rating?

___

___

Action Items

Are there any bills, debt payments, or other financial tasks I need to tackle this week?

- ○ ___
- ○ ___
- ○ ___
- ○ ___
- ○ ___

Primary Debt Payoff

Name: ___

Balance: ___ Payoff Date: ___

WEEKLY
Journal

/ /

1. Did I have any financial wins this week?

2. Did I have any financial fails this week?

3. Do I need to adjust my budget or habits this week?

4. Do I have any big financial decisions to consider this week?

WEEKLY
Journal

This week, I'm grateful for...

____

Rate This Week

1 2 3 4 5 6 7 8 9 10

Why did you give that rating?

____

____

Action Items

Are there any bills, debt payments, or other financial tasks I need to tackle this week?

- ○ ______________________________
- ○ ______________________________
- ○ ______________________________
- ○ ______________________________
- ○ ______________________________

Primary Debt Payoff

Name: ______________________________

Balance: ______________ Payoff Date: ______________

LEARNING

The acquisition of knowledge or skills through experience, study, or by being taught.

Think about what your experience has been with learning. Maybe when you were eleven a teacher made you feel stupid or a kid said that "you were slow." Maybe you've always dreaded reading. Maybe you're like I was and really struggled paying attention while learning in a school setting. Or maybe you learned best in the classroom and struggle to learn from osmosis and hands on experience.

Whatever your experience has been in the past, I don't think you would have gotten to this point in this journal if you weren't a student. The mere reading of this journal proves you are a person who desires to learn, to grow, to choose change when there is a good reason for it. Some of us have found our stride in this department, while others still feel like they need permission to try something. If you are waiting for someone to tell you "Now it's safe for you to try that new thing, or to start learning about this or that," can I give you a small encouragement? It's not up to them. They don't get to dictate what, how or when you learn. You get to choose for yourself.

Now this stance might seem privileged, arrogant or over-the-top to you. But last I checked, this kinda game changing thing called the internet is available to all, right at our fingertips. If I listed off the things that I've fixed in my house simply from watching YouTube videos, you might think I have a PhD in like six different fields. And you know what's extra neat? No one had to give me permission to learn how to fix my washing machine, learn how to flip items on Craigslist, learn to lose 80lbs in under a year by switching my eating and exercise habits, learn how to network and build a career, or even learn how to become Debt Free. All that was required is that I choose to learn and to act. Through books, podcasts, conversations, experiences, and yes, even blogs and videos I found on social media and the internet at large, I sought knowledge and wisdom beyond what I had in an effort to change my life. And you can too. Embrace your newly acquired understanding of finance and experiment, make adjustments as needed, and take charge of your own life.

If you are this far into your Debt Free Journey and you feel like an imposter, or the aunt you see every other New Years Eve has questioned why you're getting out of debt, or you feel a little unequipped to handle some of the challenges you're facing, it's okay. Chances are you don't have all the answers, and you probably never will. Same goes for all of us. But you do have the option to keep learning. To keep seeking and choosing what seems to be the next right step. No one can take that away from you except yourself.

MONTHLY
Review

/ /

1. Review last month's budget. Did anything catch me off guard or not go as planned last month?

2. Layout next month's budget. Do any categories need to change or are there any special considerations (birthdays, trips, events, expenses) this coming month?

Progress Review

How much did I pay toward debt this month?

____

What's the total amount I've paid toward debt?

____

How much debt do I have left until I'm Debt Free?

____

When is my Debt Free Date?

____

WEEKLY
Journal

/ /

1. Did I have any financial wins this week?

2. Did I have any financial fails this week?

3. Do I need to adjust my budget or habits this week?

4. Do I have any big financial decisions to consider this week?

WEEKLY
Journal

This week, I'm grateful for...

____

Rate This Week

1 2 3 4 5 6 7 8 9 10

Why did you give that rating?

____

____

Action Items

Are there any bills, debt payments, or other financial tasks I need to tackle this week?

- ○ ______________________________
- ○ ______________________________
- ○ ______________________________
- ○ ______________________________
- ○ ______________________________

Primary Debt Payoff

Name: ______________________________

Balance: ______________ Payoff Date: ______________

WEEKLY
Journal

/ /

1. Did I have any financial wins this week?

2. Did I have any financial fails this week?

3. Do I need to adjust my budget or habits this week?

4. Do I have any big financial decisions to consider this week?

WEEKLY
Journal

This week, I'm grateful for...

____

Rate This Week

1 2 3 4 5 6 7 8 9 10

Why did you give that rating?

____

____

Action Items

Are there any bills, debt payments, or other financial tasks I need to tackle this week?

○ ______________________________

○ ______________________________

○ ______________________________

○ ______________________________

○ ______________________________

Primary Debt Payoff

Name: ______________________________

Balance: ______________ Payoff Date: ______________

WEEKLY
Journal

/ /

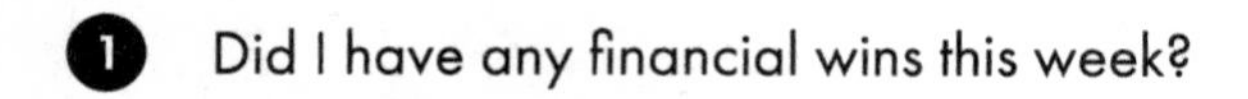

1. Did I have any financial wins this week?

2. Did I have any financial fails this week?

3. Do I need to adjust my budget or habits this week?

4. Do I have any big financial decisions to consider this week?

WEEKLY
Journal

This week, I'm grateful for...

____

Rate This Week

1 2 3 4 5 6 7 8 9 10

Why did you give that rating?

____

____

Action Items

Are there any bills, debt payments, or other financial tasks I need to tackle this week?

- ○ ______________________________
- ○ ______________________________
- ○ ______________________________
- ○ ______________________________
- ○ ______________________________

Primary Debt Payoff

Name: ______________________________

Balance: ______________ Payoff Date: ______________

WEEKLY

Journal

/ /

1. Did I have any financial wins this week?

2. Did I have any financial fails this week?

3. Do I need to adjust my budget or habits this week?

4. Do I have any big financial decisions to consider this week?

WEEKLY
Journal

This week, I'm grateful for...

____

Rate This Week

1 2 3 4 5 6 7 8 9 10

Why did you give that rating?

____

____

Action Items

Are there any bills, debt payments, or other financial tasks I need to tackle this week?

- ○ ______________________________
- ○ ______________________________
- ○ ______________________________
- ○ ______________________________
- ○ ______________________________

Primary Debt Payoff

Name: ______________________________

Balance: ______________ Payoff Date: ______________

PLANNING

The process of making a detailed proposal for doing or achieving something.

"If you fail to plan, you've planned to fail."
- Benjamin Franklin

No matter what your end goal is, it must be preceded by a well-considered, realistic plan. If your goal is to earn a Bachelor's degree in Business Management, you must have a plan that guides you through key decisions from your starting point to your desired destination. Your roadmap might look like: applying for schools that offer your major, identifying which classes to take and in what order, calculating costs associated with school and living expenses, determining how you'll fund your education and establishing your desired timeline for graduating.

A plan is not saying, "I want to get out of debt." That is merely an expressed dream, desire or hope. Merely saying, "I want to be in Hawaii." doesn't actually get your feet in the sand! Your plan is the roadmap you build to achieve that dream, desire or hope. It must also be realistic and specific. If you say, "I am going to run a marathon next week." when you haven't been on a run in six years, it's not likely you'll cross the finish line. A plan must consider all the steps, risks, obstacles, and curveballs depending on the route you take. When you set a plan, you must consider your starting point and the resources you have at your disposal and then determine exactly where you are trying to go. From there, you can assess the difficulty, how long it might take, what resources you're currently lacking, and the step-by-step directions to get to your desired destination.

While it's crucial to have a plan in order to reach and maintain your goal, the best plan is completely useless when it's not met with action. In the famous words of Pablo Picasso, "Our goals can only be reached through the vehicle of a plan, in which we must fervently believe, and upon which we must vigorously act. There is no other route to success."

You might have the best plan to achieve your Business Management degree but if it's not coupled with fervent belief and vigorous action towards that end goal, you'll be more likely to give up en route. You might have the best plan to become Debt Free, but if you don't believe that becoming Debt Free is worth all the big and small sacrifices along the way, and if you don't remain steadfast and disciplined with the necessary action steps to achieve your end goal, you are not likely to succeed.

As you continue on your Debt Free Journey, remember the plan you set out for yourself. Yes, there will be obstacles. There will be unexpected expenses and changes in circumstances. You will have small failures along the way. But don't let these derail the plan you laid out. Take your losses in stride and use them as learning opportunities so you can be better prepared when you face them again. If you truly desire to live Debt Free, know that you won't get there, or stay there, without sticking to a well-considered, realistic plan.

MONTHLY
Review

/ /

1. Review last month's budget. Did anything catch me off guard or not go as planned last month?

2. Layout next month's budget. Do any categories need to change or are there any special considerations (birthdays, trips, events, expenses) this coming month?

Progress Review

How much did I pay toward debt this month?

____

What's the total amount I've paid toward debt?

____

How much debt do I have left until I'm Debt Free?

____

When is my Debt Free Date?

____

LOOK AT YOU GO!

Six months of focused intent toward paying off debt. You should be proud of yourself! Momentum is on your side and your goal of becoming Debt Free should become more clear with each month. Remember your *why* from the beginning of the journal and why you started this journey in the first place. Keep going!

Idea: *Exercise your generosity muscles and set aside $50 to give away this month. Maybe leave a super generous tip, anonymously send a gift to a friend, or pay for someone's meal at a restaurant. You can practice generosity however you want, but I would encourage you to do it anonymously and in a manner that tangibly blesses someone. After all, we are blessed to be a blessing.*

QUARTERLY
Check-in

/ /

100% $

75% $

50% $

25% $

Debt Free Date

____

WEEKLY
Journal

/ /

1. Did I have any financial wins this week?

2. Did I have any financial fails this week?

3. Do I need to adjust my budget or habits this week?

4. Do I have any big financial decisions to consider this week?

WEEKLY
Journal

This week, I'm grateful for...

____

Rate This Week

1 2 3 4 5 6 7 8 9 10

Why did you give that rating?

____

____

Action Items

Are there any bills, debt payments, or other financial tasks I need to tackle this week?

- ○ ______________________________
- ○ ______________________________
- ○ ______________________________
- ○ ______________________________
- ○ ______________________________

Primary Debt Payoff

Name: ______________________________

Balance: ______________ Payoff Date: ______________

WEEKLY
Journal

/ /

1. Did I have any financial wins this week?

2. Did I have any financial fails this week?

3. Do I need to adjust my budget or habits this week?

4. Do I have any big financial decisions to consider this week?

WEEKLY
Journal

This week, I'm grateful for...

____

Rate This Week

1 2 3 4 5 6 7 8 9 10

Why did you give that rating?

____

____

Action Items

Are there any bills, debt payments, or other financial tasks I need to tackle this week?

- ○ ______________________________
- ○ ______________________________
- ○ ______________________________
- ○ ______________________________
- ○ ______________________________

Primary Debt Payoff

Name: ______________________________

Balance: ______________ Payoff Date: ______________

WEEKLY
Journal

/ /

1. Did I have any financial wins this week?

2. Did I have any financial fails this week?

3. Do I need to adjust my budget or habits this week?

4. Do I have any big financial decisions to consider this week?

WEEKLY
Journal

This week, I'm grateful for...

____

Rate This Week

1 2 3 4 5 6 7 8 9 10

Why did you give that rating?

____

____

Action Items

Are there any bills, debt payments, or other financial tasks I need to tackle this week?

- ○ ____
- ○ ____
- ○ ____
- ○ ____
- ○ ____

Primary Debt Payoff

Name: ____

Balance: ____________________ Payoff Date: ____________________

WEEKLY
Journal

/ /

1. Did I have any financial wins this week?

2. Did I have any financial fails this week?

3. Do I need to adjust my budget or habits this week?

4. Do I have any big financial decisions to consider this week?

WEEKLY
Journal

This week, I'm grateful for...

____

Rate This Week

1 2 3 4 5 6 7 8 9 10

Why did you give that rating?

____

____

Action Items

Are there any bills, debt payments, or other financial tasks I need to tackle this week?

- ○ ____
- ○ ____
- ○ ____
- ○ ____
- ○ ____

Primary Debt Payoff

Name: ____

Balance: ________________ Payoff Date: ________________

PATIENCE

The capacity to accept or tolerate delay or suffering without getting upset; quiet, steady perseverance or diligence.

There is no such thing as a "fast-pass" for life. Pardon the Disneyland example, but I have a three year old. Just like the best rides at Disneyland have the longest lines, some of the best things in my life have had the longest wait-times. And as much as I wish there was some kind of "fast-pass" for becoming Debt Free, it's the patient and persistent commitment to the end goal that has kept us from stepping out of line. And yes, the reward is quite the ride.

Think about something you're currently waiting for or have had to wait for in your life. Maybe it's waiting for that promotion, waiting for the right girl or guy to come along, waiting on a positive pregnancy test, waiting for your baby to finally sleep through the night, waiting to heal from an injury, or waiting to take that trip on your bucket list. Do you remember how it felt when you were finally on the other side of all that waiting, sacrificing, and persevering and at last you got to celebrate and enjoy your long awaited desire? And if you reflect back on your journey, marked by delayed gratification, might you see all the little blessings, lessons learned, and perspectives shifted while you were waiting in line? My hope is that this journal helps you realize more of those blessings during the journey rather than once you've finally reached your destination.

Quick story. We had just become Debt Free and my wife and I had this dream of traveling to Europe. Our eagerness to pursue this dream could have easily pushed us back into debt, but instead of impatiently funding our trip on a credit card, we devised a plan. Our goal was to pay for the trip with cash so we determined the cost of the trip, established our timeline for saving that amount, and then adjusted our monthly budget accordingly. We picked up side jobs, sold personal belongings, worked extra hours and made short term sacrifices all in service of our end goal. After a year of patiently sticking to our plan, we ended up saving $7,500 cash for a fifteen day trip to Europe with our best friends.

It was one of the best rides of our lives. I wish I could accurately explain to you what those two weeks felt like. The wine was richer, the Eiffel Tower more majestic, the rolling Scottish hills greener, and yes, the gelato was somehow even creamier. We were fully embracing our dream trip without worrying about how we were going to pay for it later. We felt free. All of our planning, sacrificing, and delayed gratification, allowed us the freedom to fully enjoy a dream we had patiently worked so hard for.

On your Debt Free Journey you will constantly be faced with situations that test your patience and tempt you to spend money you don't have with the lure of immediate gratification. Unfortunately, this is where many people's Debt Free Journey ends. But you have this journal to hold you accountable. Stay patient; stay the course.

MONTHLY

Review

/ /

1. Review last month's budget. Did anything catch me off guard or not go as planned last month?

2. Layout next month's budget. Do any categories need to change or are there any special considerations (birthdays, trips, events, expenses) this coming month?

Progress Review

How much did I pay toward debt this month?

____

What's the total amount I've paid toward debt?

____

How much debt do I have left until I'm Debt Free?

____

When is my Debt Free Date?

____

WEEKLY
Journal

/ /

1. Did I have any financial wins this week?

2. Did I have any financial fails this week?

3. Do I need to adjust my budget or habits this week?

4. Do I have any big financial decisions to consider this week?

WEEKLY
Journal

This week, I'm grateful for...

____

Rate This Week

1 2 3 4 5 6 7 8 9 10

Why did you give that rating?

____

____

Action Items

Are there any bills, debt payments, or other financial tasks I need to tackle this week?

○ ______________________________

○ ______________________________

○ ______________________________

○ ______________________________

○ ______________________________

Primary Debt Payoff

Name: ______________________________

Balance: ______________ Payoff Date: ______________

WEEKLY
Journal

/ /

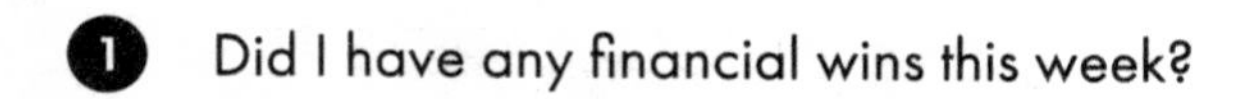

1. Did I have any financial wins this week?

2. Did I have any financial fails this week?

3. Do I need to adjust my budget or habits this week?

4. Do I have any big financial decisions to consider this week?

WEEKLY
Journal

This week, I'm grateful for...

____

Rate This Week

1 2 3 4 5 6 7 8 9 10

Why did you give that rating?

____

____

Action Items

Are there any bills, debt payments, or other financial tasks I need to tackle this week?

- ○ ______________________________
- ○ ______________________________
- ○ ______________________________
- ○ ______________________________
- ○ ______________________________

Primary Debt Payoff

Name: ______________________________

Balance: ______________ Payoff Date: ______________

WEEKLY
Journal

/ /

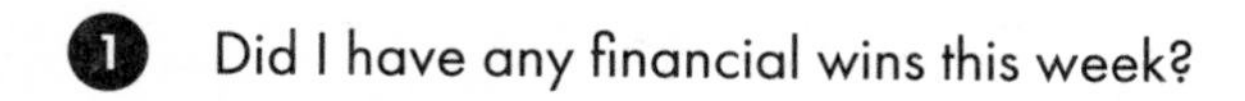

1. Did I have any financial wins this week?

2. Did I have any financial fails this week?

3. Do I need to adjust my budget or habits this week?

4. Do I have any big financial decisions to consider this week?

WEEKLY
Journal

This week, I'm grateful for...

____

Rate This Week

1 2 3 4 5 6 7 8 9 10

Why did you give that rating?

____

____

Action Items

Are there any bills, debt payments, or other financial tasks I need to tackle this week?

- ○ ____
- ○ ____
- ○ ____
- ○ ____
- ○ ____

Primary Debt Payoff

Name: ____

Balance: ____________________ Payoff Date: ____________________

WEEKLY
Journal

/ /

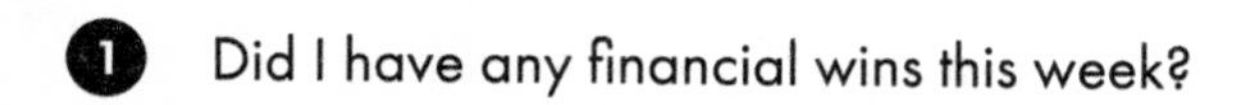

1. Did I have any financial wins this week?

2. Did I have any financial fails this week?

3. Do I need to adjust my budget or habits this week?

4. Do I have any big financial decisions to consider this week?

WEEKLY
Journal

This week, I'm grateful for...

____

Rate This Week

1 2 3 4 5 6 7 8 9 10

Why did you give that rating?

____

____

Action Items

Are there any bills, debt payments, or other financial tasks I need to tackle this week?

- ○ ____
- ○ ____
- ○ ____
- ○ ____
- ○ ____

Primary Debt Payoff

Name: ____

Balance: ____________________ Payoff Date: ____________________

SIMPLICITY

The quality of being easy to understand and within your means.

Simplicity is a word that is often misunderstood in our culture. You may associate simplicity with being unoriginal, unintelligent, incapable, boring or lacking in depth. But when it comes to your finances, simplicity means spending money in ways that you fully comprehend and value, building an intentional foundation and stewarding your own money rather than trying to "leverage" others' money to get ahead. Simplicity in your finances is being the tortoise, not the hare.

Some examples of financial simplicity might include:

- Keeping a monthly budget that covers your needs and allows excess to give, save and invest vs. creating a lifestyle above your means
- Avoiding use of credit cards or never carrying a balance month-to-month vs. buying on impulse with money you don't have
- Putting aside a portion of each paycheck to save for upcoming trips or larger expenses vs. making big decisions on a whim and determining how to pay for them later.
- Buying a house you can afford based on your actual needs vs. one you can't, basing it on how much you're approved to borrow or "historically low interest rates"
- Paying your home off early so you can live mortgage free and become financially independent earlier vs. being bound to a costly mortgage your entire life

According to a study from Experian Credit Bureau in 2019, the average American has over $90,000 in personal debts. And Millenials have increased their debts the most in the last five years, increasing by 58%. Most young American's strap themselves with student loans and credit card debt before they even launch into the real world. This "buy it now, pay for it later" mentality sets us up for a complicated financial life, always looking for a shortcut to outrun our problems rather than avoiding them in the first place by going at a pace that matches our circumstances. I don't say any of this to shame you or rub your nose in your past mistakes, I've made many of them myself, but it's essential to see our mistakes with debt for what they are and choose a different path forward.

Simplicity requires submitting yourself to parameters and living within the means of your circumstances. It allows you to approach your financial life in a manner that is aligned to your values and necessities, instead of what others expect of you. As I have counseled friends and family in their personal finances over the years, I have yet to find anyone who set out to build a complicated financial life. Instead, many have tried to take shortcuts to get ahead. They are baited by an instant gratification society that is more concerned about what it's entitled to rather than actually making a plan and working your tail off to execute the plan, slowly and intentionally, to get where you desire to be.

Choosing simplicity in finances will result in less risk, less stress, and ultimately, thinking less about money. The point in stewarding money well is not so you can spend more time thinking about it, but rather to enable you to focus on the parts of life that matter most.

MONTHLY

Review

/ /

1. Review last month's budget. Did anything catch me off guard or not go as planned last month?

2. Layout next month's budget. Do any categories need to change or are there any special considerations (birthdays, trips, events, expenses) this coming month?

Progress Review

How much did I pay toward debt this month?

____

What's the total amount I've paid toward debt?

____

How much debt do I have left until I'm Debt Free?

____

When is my Debt Free Date?

____

WEEKLY
Journal

/ /

1. Did I have any financial wins this week?

2. Did I have any financial fails this week?

3. Do I need to adjust my budget or habits this week?

4. Do I have any big financial decisions to consider this week?

WEEKLY
Journal

This week, I'm grateful for...

____

Rate This Week

1 2 3 4 5 6 7 8 9 10

Why did you give that rating?

____

____

Action Items

Are there any bills, debt payments, or other financial tasks I need to tackle this week?

- ○ ____
- ○ ____
- ○ ____
- ○ ____
- ○ ____

Primary Debt Payoff

Name: ____

Balance: ____________________ Payoff Date: ____________________

WEEKLY
Journal

/ /

1. Did I have any financial wins this week?

2. Did I have any financial fails this week?

3. Do I need to adjust my budget or habits this week?

4. Do I have any big financial decisions to consider this week?

WEEKLY
Journal

This week, I'm grateful for...

____

Rate This Week

1 2 3 4 5 6 7 8 9 10

Why did you give that rating?

____

____

Action Items

Are there any bills, debt payments, or other financial tasks I need to tackle this week?

- ○ ____________________
- ○ ____________________
- ○ ____________________
- ○ ____________________
- ○ ____________________

Primary Debt Payoff

Name: ____________________

Balance: ____________ Payoff Date: ____________

WEEKLY
Journal

/ /

1. Did I have any financial wins this week?

2. Did I have any financial fails this week?

3. Do I need to adjust my budget or habits this week?

4. Do I have any big financial decisions to consider this week?

WEEKLY
Journal

This week, I'm grateful for...

____

Rate This Week

1 2 3 4 5 6 7 8 9 10

Why did you give that rating?

____

____

Action Items

Are there any bills, debt payments, or other financial tasks I need to tackle this week?

- ○ ______________________________
- ○ ______________________________
- ○ ______________________________
- ○ ______________________________
- ○ ______________________________

Primary Debt Payoff

Name: ______________________________

Balance: ______________ Payoff Date: ______________

WEEKLY
Journal

/ /

1. Did I have any financial wins this week?

2. Did I have any financial fails this week?

3. Do I need to adjust my budget or habits this week?

4. Do I have any big financial decisions to consider this week?

WEEKLY
Journal

This week, I'm grateful for...

____

Rate This Week

1 2 3 4 5 6 7 8 9 10

Why did you give that rating?

____

____

Action Items

Are there any bills, debt payments, or other financial tasks I need to tackle this week?

- ○ ____________________________________
- ○ ____________________________________
- ○ ____________________________________
- ○ ____________________________________
- ○ ____________________________________

Primary Debt Payoff

Name: ____________________________________

Balance: ________________ Payoff Date: ________________

CONTENTMENT

Having an ease of mind, To be satisfied with, happy or joyful.

When was the last time you felt fully satisfied? When you felt like you had enough, all that you needed? In our culture of endless consumption and never-ending stimulation, contentment proves to be an extremely difficult concept to engage with. It fights against the tide of more and asks you to be satisfied in the present moment. Not after you get the promotion, buy the house, or even get out of debt. It demands that you pause, take account of all the good things in your life (shelter, air, water, food, clothes, relationships etc.), and say, "This is enough for me. I am grateful for exactly what is in front of me." As the great theologian Charles Spurgeon said, "It's not how much we have, but how much we enjoy, that makes happiness."

Now, you may be thinking, "Wait, doesn't that kind of defeat the purpose of me getting out of debt and trying to build a better future? If I could have contentment now, why would I change anything?" And that's a great question. My belief is this; contentment is not a moment in time, nor something you achieve and move on from. Contentment is a refining process that we have to consciously work toward every day.

I once heard freedom described as "not having everything that we crave, but rather, being able to surrender our cravings and being ok with it." By living within your means and stewarding your own finances, rather than giving your financial decisions over to your debtors, you are taking steps towards financial freedom. And as you take these steps towards freedom, you are aligning your income and time to the things that are most important in your life rather than requirements dictated by past mistakes. While you may be tempted along the way to take steps backwards - momentary pleasures, impulsive desires, and time-saving conveniences - don't give in, keep taking the forward steps. Be content with what you have right now, content with the journey you are on, and steadfast in the decisions you make en route to your end goal.

Living a life of contentment does not mean that you never aspire to anything beyond your present moment. It's a balance. Becoming Debt Free is a massive accomplishment, one that takes perseverance and a determination to build a better life than the one you currently have. But that doesn't mean you should be bitter or miserable while you do it. And it certainly doesn't mean that once you become Debt Free your life is perfect and that lasting happiness is achieved. Contentment is a catalyst to joy, and true joy is uncircumstantial.

To put this in perspective, when John D. Rockefeller, the richest person in American history, was asked the question, "How much money is enough?" He famously responded, "Just a little bit more." Contentment isn't achieved at a certain financial threshold, but rather by shifting your mindset to enjoy how much you already have. As Socrates wisely said, "He who is not contented with what he has, would not be contented with what he would like to have." Your goal of becoming Debt Free doesn't equate to future contentment. Be excited and determined to achieve your goal of becoming Debt Free, but don't let where you want to be blind you to where you are and what you have right now.

MONTHLY

Review

/ /

1. Review last month's budget. Did anything catch me off guard or not go as planned last month?

2. Layout next month's budget. Do any categories need to change or are there any special considerations (birthdays, trips, events, expenses) this coming month?

Progress Review

How much did I pay toward debt this month?

____

What's the total amount I've paid toward debt?

____

How much debt do I have left until I'm Debt Free?

____

When is my Debt Free Date?

____

NINE MONTHS STRONG!

By this point you are a lean mean, debt-fighting machine! You've shrugged off the initial difficulty of living more frugally, stretching dollars so that you can pay just a bit more toward your debts, and hopefully you've learned the power of the word "No." Making it this far is an accomplishment in itself. Take a moment to catch your breath and gather yourself to keep pushing toward your goal of becoming Debt Free!

Idea: *What's an experience you have been dreaming of lately? Maybe it's eating at the posh restaurant in town, getting a massage at the spa, taking your kid to the local amusement park for the day or having a night away with your significant other. Whatever it is, consider pausing to make a memory and put this dream into this month's budget.*

QUARTERLY

Check-in

/ /

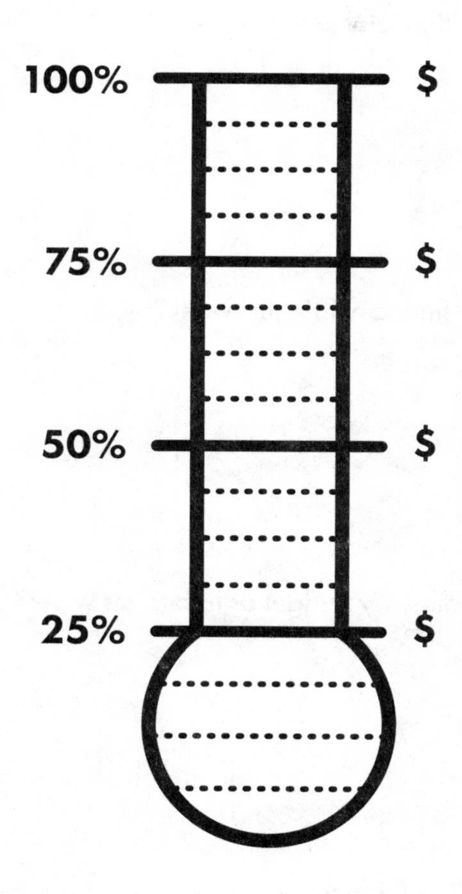

Total Debt Paid

Debt Free Date

WEEKLY

Journal

/ /

1. Did I have any financial wins this week?

2. Did I have any financial fails this week?

3. Do I need to adjust my budget or habits this week?

4. Do I have any big financial decisions to consider this week?

WEEKLY
Journal

This week, I'm grateful for...

___

Rate This Week

1 2 3 4 5 6 7 8 9 10

Why did you give that rating?

___

___

Action Items

Are there any bills, debt payments, or other financial tasks I need to tackle this week?

- ○ ___
- ○ ___
- ○ ___
- ○ ___
- ○ ___

Primary Debt Payoff

Name: ___

Balance: ___ Payoff Date: ___

WEEKLY
Journal

/ /

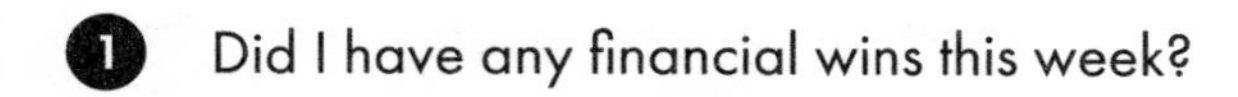

1. Did I have any financial wins this week?

2. Did I have any financial fails this week?

3. Do I need to adjust my budget or habits this week?

4. Do I have any big financial decisions to consider this week?

WEEKLY
Journal

This week, I'm grateful for...

____

Rate This Week

1 2 3 4 5 6 7 8 9 10

Why did you give that rating?

____

____

Action Items

Are there any bills, debt payments, or other financial tasks I need to tackle this week?

- ○ ____
- ○ ____
- ○ ____
- ○ ____
- ○ ____

Primary Debt Payoff

Name: ____

Balance: ____________________ Payoff Date: ____________________

WEEKLY
Journal

/ /

1. Did I have any financial wins this week?

2. Did I have any financial fails this week?

3. Do I need to adjust my budget or habits this week?

4. Do I have any big financial decisions to consider this week?

WEEKLY
Journal

This week, I'm grateful for...

____

Rate This Week

1 2 3 4 5 6 7 8 9 10

Why did you give that rating?

____

____

Action Items

Are there any bills, debt payments, or other financial tasks I need to tackle this week?

- ○ ____
- ○ ____
- ○ ____
- ○ ____
- ○ ____

Primary Debt Payoff

Name: ____

Balance: ____________________ Payoff Date: ____________________

WEEKLY
Journal

/ /

1. Did I have any financial wins this week?

2. Did I have any financial fails this week?

3. Do I need to adjust my budget or habits this week?

4. Do I have any big financial decisions to consider this week?

WEEKLY
Journal

This week, I'm grateful for...

____

Rate This Week

1 2 3 4 5 6 7 8 9 10

Why did you give that rating?

____

____

Action Items

Are there any bills, debt payments, or other financial tasks I need to tackle this week?

- ○ ____
- ○ ____
- ○ ____
- ○ ____
- ○ ____

Primary Debt Payoff

Name: ____

Balance: ____________________ Payoff Date: ____________________

GENEROSITY

The quality or act of being kind, charitable and generous to others.

This might seem like an odd principle to discuss while you're trying to dig your way out of debt. I know, it seems contradictory to consider giving away a penny when you're squeezing every penny you can find to get out of a messy situation...but hear me out.

My personal and family's chosen faith is Christianity, and in this tradition, it is customary to give regularly to the local church. This money helps support the needs of those in the church, the local community, and even people in need around the globe. While we were getting out of debt, we were not in a consistent rhythm of giving as it felt counterintuitive to our goal. It wasn't until after we became Debt Free and saved our Emergency Fund, that we began giving regularly. Reflecting back, I wish we had started this practice while we were on our journey, rather than waiting until after we had reached Debt Freedom.

What we found after we began to give regularly is that our hearts toward others changed along with our giving habits. The more we gave freely to others, the more free we felt. We experienced freedom from the burden of life being all about us. Freedom from feeling like personal finance is about being completely independent from others. Freedom from self destructive individualism. Not only did we feel freedom for ourselves, we became more aware of all the times we had benefited from others generosity in the past.

Have you ever benefited from another person's generosity? Has anyone ever bought you a coffee or made you a meal? What about something bigger? Maybe you received an anonymous scholarship for a program, camp or even school? Or perhaps someone supported your family through a difficult season? How did that make you feel? Cared for, looked after, known? My point is this, there are many ways to practice generosity. It might be a small act of kindness and selflessness or a monumental gesture that provides hope during a hard time. Regardless of the scale, your generosity will benefit and bless others, while also producing gratitude and joy in your own heart.

Budgeting for generosity each month will keep you mindful of the needs of others while pressing on towards your goal. While this may temporarily slow down your debt payoff, it will refresh your own life and cultivate a healthy relationship with the money you steward.

"A generous person will prosper; whoever refreshes others will be refreshed." - Proverbs 11:25

MONTHLY

Review

/ /

1. Review last month's budget. Did anything catch me off guard or not go as planned last month?

2. Layout next month's budget. Do any categories need to change or are there any special considerations (birthdays, trips, events, expenses) this coming month?

Progress Review

How much did I pay toward debt this month?

____

What's the total amount I've paid toward debt?

____

How much debt do I have left until I'm Debt Free?

____

When is my Debt Free Date?

____

WEEKLY
Journal

/ /

1. Did I have any financial wins this week?

2. Did I have any financial fails this week?

3. Do I need to adjust my budget or habits this week?

4. Do I have any big financial decisions to consider this week?

WEEKLY
Journal

This week, I'm grateful for...

____

Rate This Week

1 2 3 4 5 6 7 8 9 10

Why did you give that rating?

____

____

Action Items

Are there any bills, debt payments, or other financial tasks I need to tackle this week?

- ○ ____
- ○ ____
- ○ ____
- ○ ____
- ○ ____

Primary Debt Payoff

Name: ____

Balance: ____________________ Payoff Date: ____________________

WEEKLY
Journal

/ /

1. Did I have any financial wins this week?

2. Did I have any financial fails this week?

3. Do I need to adjust my budget or habits this week?

4. Do I have any big financial decisions to consider this week?

WEEKLY
Journal

This week, I'm grateful for...

____

Rate This Week

1 2 3 4 5 6 7 8 9 10

Why did you give that rating?

____

____

Action Items

Are there any bills, debt payments, or other financial tasks I need to tackle this week?

- ○ ______________________________
- ○ ______________________________
- ○ ______________________________
- ○ ______________________________
- ○ ______________________________

Primary Debt Payoff

Name: ______________________________

Balance: ______________ Payoff Date: ______________

WEEKLY
Journal

/ /

1. Did I have any financial wins this week?

2. Did I have any financial fails this week?

3. Do I need to adjust my budget or habits this week?

4. Do I have any big financial decisions to consider this week?

WEEKLY
Journal

This week, I'm grateful for...

____

Rate This Week

1 2 3 4 5 6 7 8 9 10

Why did you give that rating?

____

____

Action Items

Are there any bills, debt payments, or other financial tasks I need to tackle this week?

- ○ ____
- ○ ____
- ○ ____
- ○ ____
- ○ ____

Primary Debt Payoff

Name: ____

Balance: ____________________ Payoff Date: ____________________

WEEKLY
Journal

/ /

1. Did I have any financial wins this week?

2. Did I have any financial fails this week?

3. Do I need to adjust my budget or habits this week?

4. Do I have any big financial decisions to consider this week?

WEEKLY
Journal

This week, I'm grateful for...

Rate This Week

1 2 3 4 5 6 7 8 9 10

Why did you give that rating?

Action Items

Are there any bills, debt payments, or other financial tasks I need to tackle this week?

- ○
- ○
- ○
- ○
- ○

Primary Debt Payoff

Name: ______________________

Balance: __________ Payoff Date: __________

DESIRE

A strong craving to have something; a longing for something to happen.

We live in a culture of instant gratification. If you have a craving for that Chick-Fil-A Spicy Deluxe with waffle fries and a milkshake, you don't even have to leave your house; someone will just bring it to you. Maybe your friend posts about that new movie or show they loved. There are several ways to stream that exact movie within five minutes. Need toilet paper, groceries, a new bicycle, some fresh sneakers? Within a few days (or even a few hours) Amazon will deliver it to your doorstep.

While many of these innovations can make life more convenient, they often have an overlooked downside. These conveniences make it easier to say yes to your impulsive desires. To your cravings. They give you the option to instantly satiate a fleeting feeling or thought, even if you don't actually value whatever that thing is. In many ways, we've lost the ability to say no. No to ourselves. No to our desires. And no to others.

Our generation, now more than ever, is easily influenced by this insatiable pursuit of instant gratification. This is a huge roadblock for so many on their Debt Free Journey. It can throw you off budget or make you feel like you will never make any meaningful progress. It can easily be the difference between living off of $3,000 a month and $5,000 a month. Remember at the beginning of this journal, when you wrote your *why*? That small but powerful statement is the starting point of fighting the adversary of instant gratification. Your *why* is your deepest desire. It has to be more powerful than the urge to satiate your strongest desire - impulsive cravings that can dictate your life if you let them. Your *why* will fuel your willpower and remind you that the sacrifices to become Debt Free are worth it. Because you are never going back to the way you used to live.

On this journey to become Debt Free, there will be a thousand little decisions that could knock you off course. It's a promise. And to actually achieve freedom from debt, you are going to need to practice taming your desires. To learn how to say no. Often. You will miss some hangouts. You might not have the latest devices. Your clothes might be from a few seasons ago (heaven forbid...) You might not take that beach trip this year. But there is good news.

The goal isn't to say no to everything forever; it's to actually put you in right relationship with what you value. It doesn't mean you can never eat a meal out again, or buy a pair of shoes you really want, or grab coffee or a drink with a friend. It means you need to do it on purpose, with intent and in line with your larger goal of becoming Debt Free. Not as an impulse or as a result of boredom. This practice of taming desire doesn't just help you get out of debt, it helps you to actually live a life you value and to not be swayed by every distraction that crosses your path. It means that in the future, you will actually be able to say yes to the right things. And when you do, you'll be able to enjoy them to the fullest.

MONTHLY

Review

/ /

1. Review last month's budget. Did anything catch me off guard or not go as planned last month?

2. Layout next month's budget. Do any categories need to change or are there any special considerations (birthdays, trips, events, expenses) this coming month?

Progress Review

How much did I pay toward debt this month?

____

What's the total amount I've paid toward debt?

____

How much debt do I have left until I'm Debt Free?

____

When is my Debt Free Date?

____

WEEKLY
Journal

/ /

1. Did I have any financial wins this week?

2. Did I have any financial fails this week?

3. Do I need to adjust my budget or habits this week?

4. Do I have any big financial decisions to consider this week?

WEEKLY
Journal

This week, I'm grateful for...

___

Rate This Week

1 2 3 4 5 6 7 8 9 10

Why did you give that rating?

___

___

Action Items

Are there any bills, debt payments, or other financial tasks I need to tackle this week?

- ○ ___
- ○ ___
- ○ ___
- ○ ___
- ○ ___

Primary Debt Payoff

Name: ___

Balance: ___ Payoff Date: ___

WEEKLY
Journal

/ /

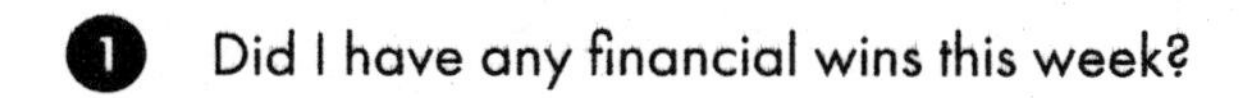

1. Did I have any financial wins this week?

2. Did I have any financial fails this week?

3. Do I need to adjust my budget or habits this week?

4. Do I have any big financial decisions to consider this week?

WEEKLY
Journal

This week, I'm grateful for...

___

Rate This Week

1 2 3 4 5 6 7 8 9 10

Why did you give that rating?

___

___

Action Items

Are there any bills, debt payments, or other financial tasks I need to tackle this week?

- ○ ___
- ○ ___
- ○ ___
- ○ ___
- ○ ___

Primary Debt Payoff

Name: ___

Balance: ___ Payoff Date: ___

WEEKLY
Journal

/ /

1. Did I have any financial wins this week?

2. Did I have any financial fails this week?

3. Do I need to adjust my budget or habits this week?

4. Do I have any big financial decisions to consider this week?

WEEKLY
Journal

This week, I'm grateful for...

Rate This Week

1 2 3 4 5 6 7 8 9 10

Why did you give that rating?

Action Items

Are there any bills, debt payments, or other financial tasks I need to tackle this week?

- ○
- ○
- ○
- ○
- ○

Primary Debt Payoff

Name: ______

Balance: ______ Payoff Date: ______

WEEKLY
Journal

/ /

1. Did I have any financial wins this week?

2. Did I have any financial fails this week?

3. Do I need to adjust my budget or habits this week?

4. Do I have any big financial decisions to consider this week?

WEEKLY
Journal

This week, I'm grateful for...

___

Rate This Week

1 2 3 4 5 6 7 8 9 10

Why did you give that rating?

___

___

Action Items

Are there any bills, debt payments, or other financial tasks I need to tackle this week?

- ○ ___
- ○ ___
- ○ ___
- ○ ___
- ○ ___

Primary Debt Payoff

Name: ___

Balance: ___ Payoff Date: ___

REFLECTION

To look back on, examine, and evaluate where you've been and where you are now.

Do you ever feel like you're just spinning your wheels? You try to do the right things, get to work on time, choose the bowl of oatmeal over the Cinnamon Toast Crunch, and you even round up the dollar at the grocery store to contribute to the local children's hospital. But despite all these little good decisions, you still feel like you're no further ahead than you were a year ago or even ten years ago. You look on Instagram and see your friend Jill bought a new house, she drives a nicer car than you and her family even has matching Christmas pajamas. Her life must be so much better than yours...

When you compare your life to others, it can be a slippery slope of discouragement, leading to discontentment, leading to doubt. This comparison might tempt you to abandon your deepest desires, your values, and your goal of becoming Debt Free. When you catch yourself in the comparison game, remind yourself that you don't get to see their whole picture nor do they get to see yours. Remind yourself that all the sacrifices you've made on your Debt Free Journey have been investments towards your end goal. Remind yourself of how far you've come! One great way to do this is by comparing yourself to...yourself. This is where reflection and reviewing progress comes in.

When you're in the moment, the small wins feel small. But when you pause to reflect on them, they often represent significant, life changing progress. Progress that reminds you how far you've come and that fuels you to keep reaching further. This is why setting goals is so helpful. When you reach your goals, you know you've gotten there on purpose and that you had to journey a long way to reach that finish line. You can take pride in the work you've done.

At this point, you are a year into this journey. Maybe you feel exhausted, over it, or like you aren't doing a good enough job. Or maybe you're patting yourself on the back for the tremendous progress you've made towards your goal. Either way, think back to where you started. Did you even have a budget? If so, did you actually follow it? Did you know what debts you had or what they were costing you each month? Did you know how to say no to your own cravings or to others? Did you think it was actually possible for anyone to become Debt Free, let alone you?

I'd bet that after one year, you've made more financial progress than you have in your entire life. You've been more intentional. You've freed up more cash. You've taken control of some bad habits. You're starting to feel the freedom you desired when you first started this journey. I hope the completion of this journal feels like a massive accomplishment, because it is! You didn't give up, you stayed consistent and patient, you learned a lot, you became more disciplined, and you are so much closer to finally becoming Debt Free. Well done! In the next section, we're going to take a moment to pause and reflect on exactly how far you've come. I hope this gets you excited about all the progress you've made!

MONTHLY
Review

/ /

1. Review last month's budget. Did anything catch me off guard or not go as planned last month?

2. Layout next month's budget. Do any categories need to change or are there any special considerations (birthdays, trips, events, expenses) this coming month?

Progress Review

How much did I pay toward debt this month?

____

What's the total amount I've paid toward debt?

____

How much debt do I have left until I'm Debt Free?

____

When is my Debt Free Date?

____

Year in Review

Introduction

You did it! You have shown an immense amount of discipline and stick-to-itiveness to get to this point. Way to go!

This is a big checkpoint and should be marked by celebration for how much progress you've made. Let's use this moment to pause, take a deep breath and look back on all you've accomplished this year. In this next section You will recap what debts you've paid off, update your Net Worth, calculate how much you've paid toward debt in total and determine how close you are to becoming Debt Free.

1. **Debt Payoff Review.** Let's look back at the Debt section in the beginning of the journal to see all those debts you've paid off and put them in one place.

2. **Total Debt Paid.** Add up all the individual debts you've paid and determine how much total debt you've paid throughout this year. We will also look at your remaining debt balance.

3. **Net Worth Update.** Take a look at where your Net Worth started this year, where it's at today and how much it's changed in just one year.

"It's never too late to become who you want to be. I hope you live a life that you're proud of, and if you find that you're not, I hope you have the strength to start over."

F SCOTT FITZGERALD

YEAR IN REVIEW

Debt

/ /

Debt Payoff Review

Total up each paid off debt and the total amount you've paid toward debt this year. To complete this section, reference your list of debts in the *Debt* section at the beginning of the journal and carry them over to this page. List the starting balance, new balance and how much has been paid off this year.

	Name	Starting Balance	New Balance	Paid Off
1.				
2.				
3.				
4.				
5.				
6.				
7.				
8.				
9.				
10.				
11.				
12.				
13.				
14.				

YEAR IN REVIEW

Debt

	Name	Starting Balance	New Balance	Paid Off
15.				
16.				
17.				
18.				
19.				
20.				
21.				
22.				
23.				
24.				
25.				
26.				

Yearly Debt Review

Total Starting Debt ______________________

Total Debt Paid ______________________

Remaining Debt Balance ______________________

Debt Free Date ______________________

YEAR IN REVIEW

Assets

/ /

Assets List

Update the estimated value for each of your assets and determine the total value.

	Name	Est. Value
1.		
2.		
3.		
4.		
5.		
6.		
7.		
8.		
9.		
10.		
11.		
12.		
13.		
14.		

Total Assets Value

____

YEAR IN REVIEW

Net Worth

Subtract

Remaining Debt Balance

____

From

Total Assets Value

____

To Find Your

Updated Net Worth

____

Subtract

Beginning Net Worth

____

From

Updated Net Worth

____

To Find Your

Net Worth Differential

____

YOU DID IT!

Congratulations! Seriously, completing this journal is no-joke! Being intentional toward personal finances for an **entire year** is a huge accomplishment and is just the beginning, my friend. At this point, you have either made a big leap forward in your Debt Free Journey or have reached the massive milestone of actually becoming Debt Free! Regardless of which camp you fall in, you should be immensely proud of yourself. And if you haven't already, share your accomplishment with a close friend! This moment should be marked by celebration with those who care about you most.

Here's to continuing the journey.

Sincerely,
Daniel Meichtry

YEAR IN REVIEW

Check-in

/ /

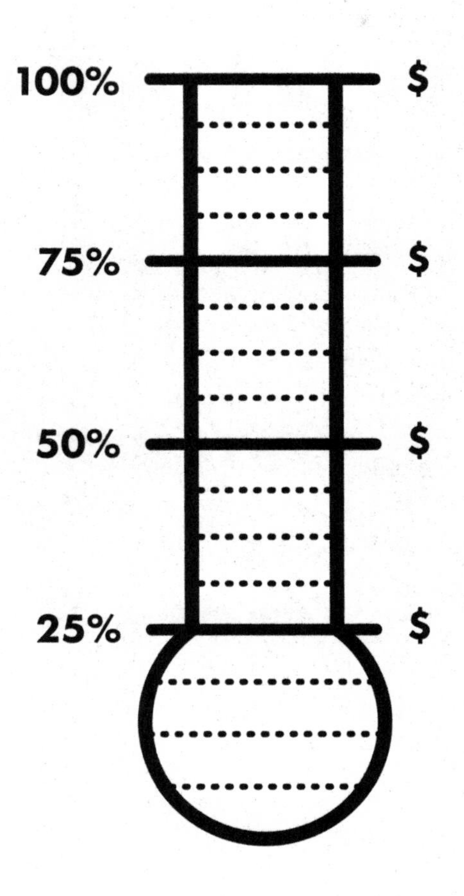

Debt Free Date

Need another journal for yourself or a friend?

If Debt Free Journal has been helpful for you, can I ask you to do something? If you are still working to pay off your debt, don't give up! Stick with this process by picking up a fresh, new journal. And if Debt Free Journal has been a helpful tool for you, please consider giving it as a gift to someone in your life that you think might benefit from it.

As a gift to you for being a boss and finishing this journal, take 10% off your next journal order with code: THANKYOU10 at checkout. My small way of saying well done!

NOTES

NOTES

NOTES

NOTES

NOTES

NOTES

NOTES

NOTES

NOTES

NOTES

NOTES

ISBN 978-0-9978240-3-2
53000>
9 780997 824032